SELAH

... pause and think about it!

Selah. ... pause and think about it!
First published June 2006
Second printing November 2006

Houston, Brian
ISBN 09752060 2 8

Scripture quotations used in this book are from the following sources
and used with permission:
New King James Version (NKJV). Copyright © 1982, 1992 by Thomas
Nelson, Inc. Used by permission. All rights reserved.
Amplified Bible (AMP). Old Testament Copyright © 1965, 1987 by the
Zondervan Corporation. New Testament copyright © 1958, 1987 by
the Lockman Foundation. Used by permission.
New International Version (NIV). Copyright © 1973,1978, 1984
International Bible Society. All rights reserved throughout the world.
Used by permission of International Bible Society.

Bold emphasis in certain scriptures are the author's own.

Photographs by Bobbie Houston, Joel Houston, Ben Houston, Laura
Houston, Darren Kitto, David Anderson and others.

Layout and design by Daryl-Anne Le Roux.

Printed by Pegasus Printing, Rosebery NSW Australia.

Published by Leadership Ministries Inc.
www. leadershipministries.com.au

SELAH

... **pause and think about it!**

BRIAN HOUSTON

Selah

Words have the power to inspire, fuel and keep us on course with destiny. But we have to take time to stop, think and reflect on them for their potency to be felt.

Within these pages, I have endeavoured to draw together a collection of statements, sayings and thoughts that have helped define my life, and shaped the culture of Hillsong Church. Some are original, forged and formed from more than 30 years of ministry and over five decades of life, whilst some have been gleaned or borrowed from others.

I encourage you, in the busyness of life, to take time to pause and deliberately think on these things. My prayer is that as you do, you will be inspired and draw wisdom for your own life and future.

The Church that I See

The Church that I see is a Church of influence. A Church so large in size that the city and nation cannot ignore it. A Church growing so quickly that buildings struggle to contain the increase.

I see a Church whose heartfelt praise and worship touches Heaven and changes earth; worship which influences the praises of people throughout the earth, exalting Christ with powerful songs of faith and hope.

I see a Church whose altars are constantly filled with repentant sinners responding to Christ's call to salvation.

Yes, the Church that I see is so dependent on the Holy Spirit that nothing will stop it nor stand against it; a Church whose people are unified, praying and full of God's Spirit.

The Church that I see has a message so clear that lives are changed forever and potential is fulfilled through the power of His Word; a message beamed to the peoples of the earth through their television screens.

I see a Church so compassionate that people are drawn from impossible situations into a loving and friendly circle of hope, where answers are found and acceptance is given.

I see a people so Kingdom-minded that they will count whatever the cost and pay whatever the price to see revival sweep this land.

The Church that I see is a Church so committed to raising, training and empowering a leadership generation to reap the end-time harvest that all its ministries are consumed with this goal.

I see a Church whose head is Jesus, whose help is the Holy Spirit and whose focus is the Great Commission.

YES, THE CHURCH THAT I SEE COULD WELL BE OUR CHURCH ~ HILLSONG CHURCH.

[January 1996]

LIFE is for living.

Your life is a gift. Living your life is a choice.

'... I have come that they may have life ...' – Jesus [John 10:10]

Joel surfing – Indonesia

God-given
DESTINY positions you

in the **right place**,
at the **right time**,
with the **right people**.

A true friend is a
FRIEND to your destiny.

30 years on at Papamoa Beach, New Zealand - where we met

'He who walks with wise men will be wise ...' [Proverbs 13:20]

We're not on earth to mark time.

We're here to
make a DIFFERENCE.

Many Christians **just** live saved.
The Bible inspires us to live
CALLED.

'[He] who has saved us and called us with a holy calling, not according to our works, but according to His own purpose and grace ...' [2 Timothy 1:9]

A VISION is only as powerful as

the CAUSE it's attached to.

A vision can be personal but the Cause is bigger than any one person.

'For this cause I was born ...' – Jesus [John 18:37]

I can't imagine anything more rewarding than spending my life building

what Jesus said He would build – His Church.

'... I will build My Church and the gates of Hades will not prevail against it.' – Jesus [Matthew 16:18]

The Church is all about

GOD and PEOPLE.

Church should be

enjoyed, not endured.

A person's expectation of God

can be seen in the way they PRAY.

'You are good and You do good.' – King David [Psalm 119:68]

'No good thing will He withhold from those who walk uprightly.' [Psalm 84:11]

Leaders must ask themselves:
'Can people flourish under
my leadership?'

If they can't FLOURISH, why would they stay planted?

'Those who are planted in the house of the Lord shall flourish in the courts of our God.' [Psalm 92:13]

When God thinks gifts,
He thinks PEOPLE.

'For God so loved the world that He gave His only begotten Son ...' [John 3:16]

GENEROSITY is

a way of thinking,
 a way of seeing, and
 a way of living.

'... a generous man devises generous things, and by generosity he shall stand.' [Isaiah 32:8]

If you see a need and
you have nothing,
there is NOTHING you can do.

If you have a little,
you can help a little.

But if you have a lot,
there's a WHOLE lot you can do.

Personal wealth is not the message. It's personal effectiveness.

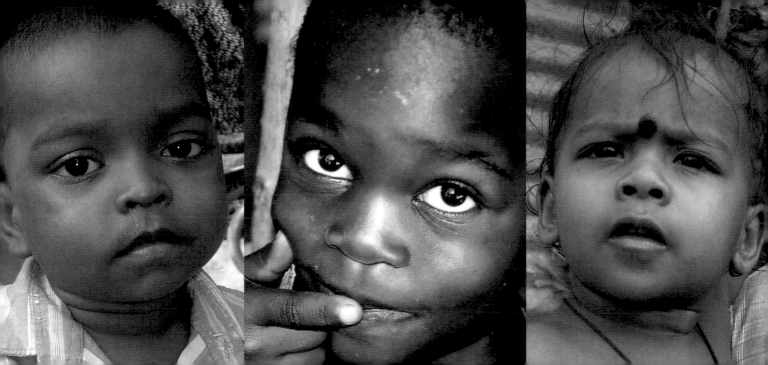

Our church will always have

more VISION than resource.

Living your life BLESSED is better

than living your life RICH.

Rich thinks, 'I have need of nothing.'   [Revelation 3:17]

Blessed thinks, 'I can be a blessing.'   [Genesis 12:2]

SPENDING is seasonal ...

GIVING is a lifestyle.

Use what's in your hand to fulfil what's in your heart.

God didn't create you one way to use you a different way.
The same God who put gifts and talents in your hand,
puts purpose in your heart.

Life's biggest battles are INTERNAL

not external.

It's not what happens TO you but what happens IN you that determines your life's outcome.

Great churches aren't built on the

gifts or talents of a few
but on the **sacrifice** of many.

You'll never come second

by putting God first.

'But seek first the kingdom of God and His righteousness, and all these things shaill be added to you.' – Jesus [Matthew 6:33]

LOVE GOD ...

PEOPLE ...

... LOVE LIFE.

ANYTHING could happen

... and it probably will!

Live with a positive expectation of the unexpected. Serving God is an adventure.

Don't try and fit Jesus into your life.

Fit your life around Jesus.

Don't allow God, family and church to compete with one another. Life is at its richest when they all flow together.

I want to preach to

people's Mondays

... not just their
Sundays.

Don't focus on
the GROWTH of the church.

Focus on
the HEALTH of the church
– because healthy things grow.

'Beloved, I pray that you may prosper in all things and be in health, just as your soul prospers.' [3 John 1: 2]

The Houston family NOT looking their best!

It's not the BIG events
that build a great family,
marriage or church,
but the everyday things.

'So teach us to number our days, that we may gain a heart of wisdom.' [Psalm 90:12]

The greatest threat to the Church
doesn't come from the outside ...

it's COMPLACENCY on the inside.

I'd rather be an artist than an art critic.
I'd rather be a movie-maker than a movie critic.
I'd rather be a musician than a music critic.
And I'd rather be a church builder than a church critic.

The same people who
dismiss the Church as being
old, empty, boring and irrelevant
criticise it for being
big, successful, young and relevant.

The message is timeless but the methods must change.

The best way to frustrate your critics

is to keep being SUCCESSFUL

at what you do.

Outlast your opposition.

No matter what happens to you in life

never develop a wounded spirit.

We'll all have opportunities to get offended, but we can choose to rise above it.

'Whoever has no rule over his own spirit is like a city broken down, without walls.' [Proverbs 25:28]

Everyone has a right to their opinion

but it's not always right to give it.

The smaller the man on the inside, the BIGGER the opinion.

EVERYTHING about you says

SOMETHING about you.

The theme of your HEART is

writing the STORY of your LIFE.

'My heart is overflowing with a good theme ...
my tongue is the pen of a ready writer.' [Psalm 45:1]

"... My help comes from the Lord..."
Psalm 121:1

One of our Compassion children.

Are you building your life around what's **wrong** with you, or what's **right** with Him?

His righteousness or your 'wrongousness'? [sic]

He has made you righteous.
[Romans 5:19]

Your **outlook** depends on
what you're looking OUT from.

'As [a man] thinks in his heart, so is he.' [Proverbs 23:7]

Your perception is as powerful as your reality.

If you STAND for nothing,

you'll fall for anything.

Are you ruled by
what MIGHT happen or
what you THINK you can't do?

NEGATIVITY holds you well below your potential.

My sister Judith

Lift your experience
to the level of your BELIEF,

rather than lowering your belief
to the level of your experience.

LOVE's greatest threat is not HATE

- it's indifference.

If you want Bible results,

you must live by
Bible principles.

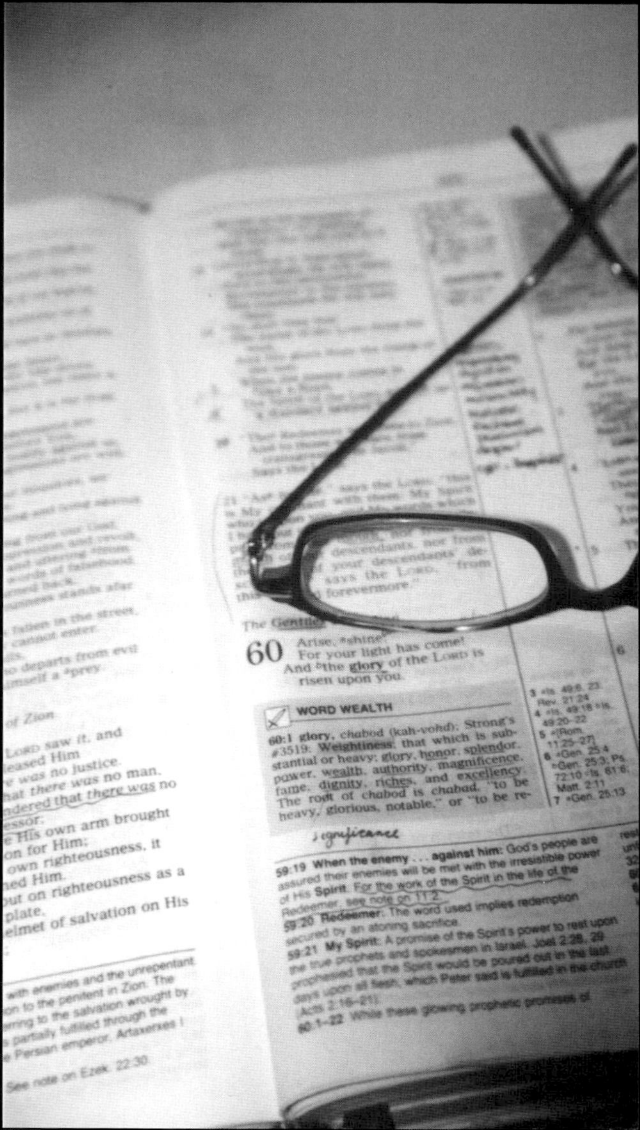

Some things are CAUGHT,
not taught.

United in a Cause - Hillsong Conference, Acer Arena.

If the people around you were dependent on your WORDS for nourishment, would they be dying of malnutrition?

'The lips of the righteous feed many ...' [Proverbs 10:21]

Increase your value
so you can accomplish in
a SINGLE DAY

what once would have taken a THOUSAND days.

'May the Lord, the God of your fathers, increase you a thousand times and bless you as He has promised!' [Deuteronomy 1:11]

'For a day in Your courts is better than a thousand.' [Psalm 84:10]

LEADERSHIP gives

people an EXAMPLE to follow.

Progress is a PROCESS –
many want the destination
but not the journey.

The Church must empower

people to LEAD

and IMPACT in every sphere of life.

[Ephesians 4:12]

HARD WORK builds a legacy for the next generation.

LAZINESS squanders the legacy of the last generation.

YOU CAN CHANGE

THE FUTURE.

Our decisions affect the generations to come.

'Blessed is the man who fears the Lord ... his descendants will be mighty on the earth ...' [Psalm 112:1,2]

It's not how well you start that counts

... it's how well you FINISH.

The **BEST** is yet to come!

Are you positioned for God's best?

For more information on resources by Brian Houston:
www.leadershipministries.com.au